50 Proven Side Hustles: Turn Your Spare Time into $1000 a Month

Wake Up and Smell the Side Hustle

Chapter 1: Why Your 9-5 Job is Killing You (And Your Dreams)

Chapter 2: The Side Hustle Mindset: Embrace Your Inner Hustler

Chapter 3: 50 Side Hustles That Actually Work

Chapter 4: From Zero to $1000: Your First Month's Gameplan

Chapter 5: Scaling Up: Turn Your Side Hustle into a Cash Cow

Chapter 6: The Dark Side of Side Hustles: What They Don't Tell You

Chapter 7: Taxes, Legalities, and Other Boring Stuff You Can't Ignore

Chapter 8: Work Smarter, Not Harder: Automation and Outsourcing

Chapter 9: The Side Hustle Lifestyle: Balancing Hustle and Life

Stop Reading, Start Hustling

Wake Up and Smell the Side Hustle

Listen up, wage slaves and dreamers! If you're reading this, you're probably sick of living paycheck to paycheck, watching your soul die a little more each day as you trudge to your mundane 9-5. Well, guess what? You're not alone, and there's a way out.

Welcome to "50 Proven Side Hustles: Turn Your Spare Time into $1000 a Month." This isn't your grandma's finance book. We're not here to tell you to clip coupons or skip your daily latte. No, we're here to show you how to grab life by the horns and milk it for all it's worth.

In this book, we're going to explore the wild world of side hustles. These aren't just cute little hobbies to keep you busy on weekends. We're talking about serious money-making ventures that can pad your wallet, fund your dreams, and maybe even set you free from the corporate hamster wheel.

But let's get one thing straight: this isn't a get-rich-quick scheme. If you're looking for a magic bullet that'll turn you into a millionaire overnight, you've picked up the wrong book. What we're offering is a no-BS guide to leveraging your skills, time, and maybe a little elbow grease to create additional income streams.

So, who the hell am I to be telling you all this? Well, I've been in your shoes. I've felt the soul-crushing weight of a dead-end job. I've stared at my bank account in despair, wondering how I'd ever afford more than ramen noodles and Netflix. But then I discovered the power of the side hustle.

Over the years, I've tried it all. I've been a dog walker, a freelance writer, an Amazon seller, and even a professional line-stander (yes, that's a real thing). Some hustles were duds, others were goldmines. And now, I'm here to share everything I've learned with you.

In the following chapters, we'll dive into 50 proven side hustles that can help you earn an extra $1000 a month. We'll talk about how to get started, how to scale up, and how to avoid the pitfalls that trip up most newbie hustlers. We'll also tackle the mindset shifts you need to make to go from wage slave to side hustle superstar.

But here's the kicker: this book isn't for everyone. If you're looking for a gentle pat on the back and reassurance that everything will be okay, you're in the wrong place. This book is for the rebels, the risk-takers, the ones who are willing to sacrifice a little comfort now for a whole lot of freedom later.

So, are you ready to stop dreaming and start doing? Are you prepared to turn your spare time into cold, hard cash? Then buckle up, buttercup. It's time to hustle.

Cap 1
Why Your 9-5 Job is Killing You (And Your Dreams)

Let's start with a hard truth: your 9-5 job is slowly killing you. Yeah, I said it. That cushy office chair? It's a death trap. That steady paycheck? It's golden handcuffs. That corner office you're eyeing? It's just a fancier cage.

Now, before you get all defensive and start listing the benefits of your oh-so-wonderful job, let's break down exactly why the traditional 9-5 grind is sucking the life out of you:

1. The Illusion of Security

Remember when your parents told you to get a good job with benefits? Well, they lied. In today's world, job security is about as real as a unicorn riding a rainbow. Companies downsize, automate, and outsource faster than you can say "unemployment benefits." That job you think is so secure? It could vanish tomorrow, leaving you high and dry.

But here's the real kicker: even if you keep your job, you're still not secure. You're at the mercy of your employer. They decide your worth, your schedule, and whether you can take time off to see your kid's school play. Is that really security, or is it just comfortable servitude?

2. TheTimeTrap

Let's do some math, shall we? You work 8 hours a day, 5 days a week. Add in your commute, and you're easily spending 50 hours a week on work-related activities. That's 2,600 hours a year, or 108 days. Over a 40-year career, that's 11.7 years of your life!

Now, what are you getting in return for this massive chunk of your existence? A paycheck that barely covers your bills? The privilege of sitting in mind-numbing meetings? The joy of office politics? Sounds like a raw deal to me.

3. TheCreativityKiller

Remember when you were a kid, full of dreams and wild ideas? What happened to that spark? Oh right, it got snuffed out by TPS reports and quarterly reviews. The 9-5 grind is a creativity killer. It forces you into a box, stifles your innovative spirit, and turns you into a corporate zombie.

Sure, some companies talk a big game about fostering creativity and innovation. But let's be real: most of the time, you're expected to color within the lines and not rock the boat. Is that really living, or just existing?

4. TheHealthHazard

Sitting is the new smoking, folks. Your 9-5 job is literally killing you, one sedentary hour at a time. Studies have shown that prolonged sitting increases your risk of heart disease, diabetes, and even certain cancers. And let's not even get started on the stress-induced health problems that come from dealing with incompetent bosses and office drama.

But it's not just your physical health at stake. The 9-5 grind takes a toll on your mental health too. Depression, anxiety, and burnout are all too common in the corporate world. Is that promotion really worth your sanity?

5. The Dream Deferral

How many times have you said, "I'll do that when I retire" or "Maybe next year"? The 9-5 life is all about deferring your dreams. You put off traveling, starting that business, writing that novel, all in the name of being a responsible adult with a steady job.

But here's the brutal truth: tomorrow isn't guaranteed. You could spend your whole life working towards a retirement that never comes. Is that a risk you're willing to take?

6. The Money Mirage

Sure, your job pays the bills. But at what cost? You're trading your time – the most precious resource you have – for a fixed amount of money. And let's be honest, for most people, that amount isn't nearly enough to live the life they want.

What's worse, you're putting all your financial eggs in one basket. If that job disappears, so does your income. In today's economy, that's a recipe for disaster.

7. The Growth Plateau

In a 9-5 job, your growth is limited. You might get the occasional training or promotion, but for the most part, you're constrained by the company's structure and needs. Your personal and professional growth takes a backseat to the company's goals.

And let's not forget about skill stagnation. In many jobs, you're doing the same tasks day in and day out. While you might become an expert in those specific tasks, you're not broadening your skill set or challenging yourself in new ways.

8. The Work-Life Imbalance

We've all heard about work-life balance, right? Well, in most 9-5 jobs, it's more like work-life domination. Your job dictates when you wake up, when you can take a vacation, even when you can use the bathroom. Your life revolves around your work schedule, leaving precious little time for family, friends, hobbies, or personal growth.

9. The Identity Crisis

Here's a fun experiment: go to a party and ask people to introduce themselves. Chances are, most will lead with their job title. "Hi, I'm John, I'm an account manager." We've become so entrenched in the 9-5 mindset that we've let our jobs become our identities. But you are so much more than your job title. Don't let your 9-5 define you.

10. The Entrepreneurial Death Knell

Last but not least, the 9-5 job is killing your entrepreneurial spirit. It's training you to be a good employee, not a successful business owner. You're learning how to follow rules, not how to make them. You're being conditioned to seek permission, not to take initiative.

So, what's the alternative? That's where side hustles come in. A side hustle allows you to:

- Create multiple income streams, reducing your financial risk
- Pursue your passions and creativity
- Learn new skills and continually grow
- Take control of your time and schedule
- Build something that's truly yours

Now, I'm not saying you should march into your boss's office tomorrow and quit (although if you do, please record it for posterity). What I am saying is that it's time to wake up and realize that your 9-5 job isn't the safe, secure path you think it is. It's a slow death trap, both for your dreams and for your potential.

In the next chapter, we'll talk about how to develop the side hustle mindset. It's time to break free from the 9-5 shackles and start building the life you really want. Are you ready to make the leap?

Cap 2

The Side Hustle Mindset: Embrace Your Inner Hustler

Alright, future moguls, it's time to rewire that corporate-conditioned brain of yours. If you want to succeed in the world of side hustles, you need to ditch the employee mindset and embrace your inner hustler. Buckle up, because this might just be the most important mindset shift of your life.

1. Ditch the Permission Mentality

First things first: stop asking for permission. In your 9-5, you're conditioned to seek approval for everything. Want to try a new approach? Ask your boss. Need to take a day off? Fill out a form. Want a raise? Wait for your annual review.

Well, guess what? In the world of side hustles, there's no one to ask permission from except yourself. You're the boss now, baby. That means you call the shots, make the decisions, and take the risks. It's liberating, but it can also be terrifying if you're used to having someone else make the big decisions.
Start small. Make decisions without consulting anyone else. Take risks in low-stakes situations. Gradually, you'll

build the confidence to make bigger moves without seeking external validation.

2. Embrace Failure as Your Best Teacher

In your 9-5, failure is often seen as a career-killer. But in the world of side hustles, failure is your best friend. Every failed attempt is a lesson learned, a step closer to success.

Did your first Etsy shop flop? Great! Now you know what doesn't work. Did your freelance gig get a bad review? Fantastic! That's valuable feedback for improvement. The only real failure is giving up or not trying at all. Develop a "fail fast, learn faster" mentality. Don't be afraid to try new things, and when (not if) you fail, dissect that failure to extract every possible lesson. Your ability to learn and adapt quickly will be your superpower in the side hustle world.

3. Time is Money (No, Seriously)

In your 9-5, you might be used to clock-watching, eagerly awaiting the end of your shift. But when you're hustling on the side, every minute counts. You need to start seeing your time as the valuable resource it is.

This doesn't mean you need to be "productive" every waking moment. It means being intentional about how you spend your time. Binge-watching the latest Netflix series? That's fine, as long as it's a conscious choice, not a default time-waster.

Start tracking your time for a week. See where your hours are going. Then, start making deliberate choices about how to allocate your time. Remember, every hour you invest in your side hustle is an hour invested in your future freedom.

4. Cultivate a Growth Mindset

In the corporate world, it's easy to fall into a fixed mindset. You have your role, your skills, your place in the hierarchy. But in the side hustle world, a growth mindset is essential.
Believe that you can learn, grow, and improve. Don't know how to build a website? You can learn. Never done freelance writing before? You can start. Think you're "not a sales person"? That's a skill you can develop.

Challenge yourself to learn something new every day. Read books, take online courses, attend workshops. Your ability to acquire new skills quickly will be a major asset in your side hustle journey.

5. Embrace the Hustle (But Don't Glorify the Grind)

Let's be clear: building a successful side hustle takes work. There will be late nights, early mornings, and sacrificed weekends. You need to be prepared to put in the effort.

But here's where I differ from some of the "hustle porn" gurus out there: don't glorify the grind for the sake of grinding. Working 20 hours a day isn't a badge of honor; it's a recipe for burnout.

Instead, focus on working smart. Prioritize high-impact activities. Learn to delegate and automate. Your goal should be to build a side hustle that gives you more freedom, not less.

6. Develop a Abundance Mindset

In the corporate world, resources often seem scarce. There's only so much budget, so many promotions, so much recognition to go around. This scarcity mindset can bleed into your side hustle efforts if you're not careful.

Instead, cultivate an abundance mindset. There are more opportunities out there than you can possibly take advantage of. There's enough success to go around. Your win doesn't have to come at someone else's expense.

This mindset shift will help you see opportunities where others see obstacles. It'll make you more willing to collaborate, to share knowledge, and to celebrate others' successes alongside your own.

7. Be Unapologetically You

In the corporate world, you often have to fit into a predefined mold. But in the side hustle world, your uniqueness is your strength. Don't be afraid to let your personality shine through in your work.

Are you irreverent? Use that in your marketing. Have a quirky sense of humor? Let it come through in your product descriptions. Passionate about a niche topic? That could be your unique selling point.

Remember, people buy from people. The more authentically you present yourself, the more you'll attract the right customers and opportunities.

8. Embrace Uncertainty

If there's one thing you can be certain of in the side hustle world, it's uncertainty. Markets change, trends shift, algorithms get updated. What worked yesterday might not work tomorrow.

Instead of fearing this uncertainty, learn to embrace it. See it as an opportunity for growth and adaptation. Develop the ability to pivot quickly when needed. Stay curious and always be on the lookout for new opportunities.

9. Develop a Problem-Solving Mindset

In your 9-5, you might be used to having support systems in place. IT department for tech issues, HR for people problems, maintenance for equipment failures. But when you're hustling on your own, you are all those departments rolled into one.

Cultivate a problem-solving mindset. Instead of getting frustrated when things go wrong (and they will), get excited about the challenge of finding a solution. This mindset will not only help you overcome obstacles in your side hustle but can also lead to new business ideas.

10. Think Long-Term

Finally, develop a long-term mindset. Your side hustle isn't just about making a quick buck (although that's nice too). It's about building something sustainable that can potentially replace your 9-5 income and give you the freedom you crave.

This means making decisions not just based on immediate gains, but on long-term growth. It means reinvesting profits back into your business. It means building relationships, not just transactions.

Think of your side hustle as planting a seed. It needs consistent care and attention to grow into a mighty oak that can support you.

Developing these mindset shifts isn't easy. You're going against years of conditioning from the traditional work world. But here's the thing: once you start thinking like a hustler, you'll start seeing opportunities everywhere. You'll start acting with more confidence, taking calculated risks, and building something truly yours.

So, how do you start cultivating this side hustle mindset? Here are some practical steps:

1. Start a "Hustle Journal": Everyday, write down one idea for a side hustle or a way to improve an existing one. They don't all have to be winners. The point is to train your brain to constantly be on the lookout for opportunities.
2. Set Audacious Goals: Don't limit yourself to what seems "realistic" based on your current situation. Set big, scary goals. Even if you don't reach them, you'll likely go further than you would have with "safe" goals.
3. Find Your Tribe: Surround yourself with other side hustlers. Join online communities, attend local meetups, or start your own mastermind group. Being around like-minded individuals will reinforce your new mindset.
4. Create a "FailureResume" Instead of hiding your failures, celebrate them. Keep a running list of things you've tried that didn't work out, and what you learned from each experience.
5. Practice Saying "No": Your time and energy are precious resources. Learn to say no to things that don't align with your goals or values. This includes social obligations, additional work

responsibilities, or even side hustle opportunities that aren't the right fit.

6. Invest in Yourself: Allocate time and money for personal development. Whether it's books, courses, conferences, or coaching, see it as an investment in your future success.

7. Develop a Morning Routine: Start your day with activities that reinforce your side hustle mindset. This could include meditation, affirmations, reading, or working on your side hustle before your day job.

8. Practice Gratitude: It's easy to get caught up in the hustle and forget to appreciate how far you've come. Take time each day to acknowledge your progress and the opportunities you have.

9. Embrace Discomfort: Regularly do things that push you out of your comfort zone. This could be as simple as striking up conversations with strangers or as bold as pitching your services to a dream client.

10. Celebrate Small Wins Don't wait for huge milestones to celebrate. Acknowledge and reward yourself for small progress. This positive reinforcement will help solidify your new mindset.

Remember, developing a side hustle mindset isn't about becoming a different person. It's about unleashing the badass entrepreneur that's been hiding inside you all along. It's about shedding the limitations that your 9-5 job and society have placed on you and embracing your full potential.

Will it be easy? Hell no. Will it be worth it? Absolutely. So,

are you ready to stop thinking like an employee and start thinking like a hustler? Are you prepared to take control of your time, your income, and your future? Then let's dive into the meat of this book – the 50 side hustles that can turn your spare time into serious cash.

But fair warning: once you start down this path, there's no going back. You'll never look at your time, your skills, or the world around you the same way again. You'll start seeing dollar signs where others see problems. You'll start dreaming bigger than you ever have before.

Welcome to the world of side hustles, my friend. It's time to embrace your inner hustler and start building the life you've always wanted. The next chapter is where the rubber meets the road. We're going to dive into 50 proven side hustles that can help you start bringing in that extra $1000 a month. Are you ready? Let's do this.

Cap 3
50 Side Hustles That Actually Work

Alright, future moguls, it's time to get down to brass tacks. We've talked about why your 9-5 is slowly killing you, and we've worked on developing that crucial side hustle mindset. Now it's time for the main event: 50 side hustles that can actually put some serious cash in your pocket.

But before we dive in, let me be crystal clear: these aren't get-rich-quick schemes or pie-in-the-sky fantasies. These are real, proven side hustles that people just like you are using right now to pad their bank accounts and build their empires. Some require specialized skills, others just need a bit of elbow grease. But all of them have the potential to generate that extra $1000 a month we're aiming for.

So, without further ado, let's dive into the world of side hustles:

1. **Freelance Writing**: Don't roll your eyes – this isn't just for English majors. If you can string a sentence together, there's money to be made. From blog posts to product descriptions, the demand for content is insatiable.

How to start: Create a portfolio (even if it's just samples), set up profiles on freelancing platforms like Upwork or Fiverr, and start pitching.

Potential earnings: $50-$500+ per article, depending on your experience and niche.

> 2. **Virtual Assistant**: Businesses are always looking for help with tasks like email management, scheduling, and data entry. If you're organized and can manage your time well, this could be your golden ticket.

How to start: List your services on VA-specific job boards or reach out directly to small business owners in your network.

Potential earnings: $15-$50+ per hour, depending on your skills and the tasks involved.

> 3. **Online Tutoring**: Got knowledge? Share it. With platforms like VIPKid and Chegg, you can teach everything from English to advanced calculus from the comfort of your couch.

How to start: Sign up on tutoring platforms, create a compelling profile, and start booking sessions.
Potential earnings: $15-$50+ per hour, depending on the subject and platform.

4. **Dropshipping**: This is the holy grail of passive income for many. You set up an online store, but the products are shipped directly from the supplier to the customer. You never touch the inventory.

How to start: Choose a niche, find suppliers on platforms like AliExpress, set up a Shopify store, and start marketing.

Potential earnings: Sky's the limit, but realistically, $500-$5000+ per month once you get the hang of it.

5. **Social Media Management**: Businesses need social media presence, but many don't have the time or know-how to manage it effectively. That's where you come in.

How to start: Build your own social media presence as a portfolio, then reach out to local businesses or look for gigs on freelancing platforms.

Potential earnings: $500-$2000+ per month per client, depending on the scope of work.

6. **Pet Sitting/Dog Walking**: If you love animals, why not get paid to hang out with them? Apps like Rover and Wag make it easy to connect with pet owners in your area.

How to start: Sign up on pet sitting platforms, create a compelling profile with photos, and start booking gigs.

Potential earnings: $20-$50+ per walk or $30-$80+ per night for pet sitting.

> 7. **Affiliate Marketing**: Promote other people's products and earn a commission on each sale. It's like being a salesperson, but without the awkward face-to-face interactions.

How to start: Choose a niche, sign up for affiliate programs (Amazon Associates is a good place to start), and create content to promote products.

Potential earnings: Varies widely, but successful affiliate marketers can make $1000+ per month.

> 8. **Flipping Items**: Buy low, sell high. It's a simple concept, but it works. From flea market finds to garage sale gems, there's money to be made in reselling.

How to start: Start with items you already own, then reinvest profits into buying more inventory. Sell on platforms like eBay, Facebook Marketplace, or Craigslist.

Potential earnings: $500-$3000+ per month, depending on your hustle and eye for deals.

> 9. **Airbnb Hosting**: Got a spare room? Make it work for you. Airbnb has made it easier than ever to become a part-time hospitality mogul.

How to start: Clean up that spare room, take some great photos, and list it on Airbnb. Be sure to check local regulations first.

Potential earnings: Varies by location, but $500-$2000+ per month is possible in many areas.

10. **Graphic Design**: From logos to social media graphics, businesses always need design work. If you've got an eye for aesthetics, this could be your ticket to side hustle success.

How to start: Build a portfolio (even if it's just mock-ups), set up profiles on freelancing platforms, and start bidding on projects.

Potential earnings: $25-$150+ per hour, depending on your skills and the complexity of the project.

11. **Podcasting**: Got something to say? Say it into a microphone and monetize it. With the right niche and marketing, podcasting can be a lucrative side hustle.

How to start: Choose a niche, invest in some basic equipment, record a few episodes, and start promoting on social media and podcast directories.

Potential earnings: Varies widely, but successful podcasters can earn $500-$10000+ per month through ads, sponsorships, and affiliate marketing.

12. **Print-on-Demand** Design t-shirts, mugs, phone cases, and more, without holding any inventory. Platforms like Printful and Redbubble handle the printing and shipping.

How to start: Create designs, set up shops on print-on-demand platforms, and start marketing your products.

Potential earnings: $500-$5000+ per month, depending on your designs and marketing efforts.

13. **Proofreading and Editing** If you've got an eye for detail and a solid grasp of grammar, this could be your calling. From academic papers to business documents, there's always a need for sharp-eyed editors.

How to start: Take a proofreading course to sharpen your skills, then look for gigs on freelancing platforms or reach out to academic institutions.

Potential earnings: $20-$50+ per hour, depending on your experience and the type of document.

14. **Voice Acting** Got a smooth voice or a talent for accents? Voice acting could be your ticket to side hustle success. From audiobooks to commercial voiceovers, there's a wide range of opportunities.

How to start: Create a demo reel, set up a profile on voice acting platforms like Voices.com, and start auditioning for gigs.

Potential earnings: $100-$500+ per hour for professional gigs, though rates can vary widely.

15. **Personal Shopping/Styling** If you've got a knack for fashion and an eye for deals, why not get paid to shop? From busy professionals to those who just hate shopping, there's a market for personal shoppers.

How to start: Build a portfolio of your own looks, network with local boutiques, and start promoting your services on social media.

Potential earnings: $50-$200+ per shopping session, plus possible commissions from stores.

16. **Online Course Creation** If you're an expert in something, why not package that knowledge into an online course? From coding to knitting, there's a market for almost every skill.

How to start: Choose your topic, create your content (video, text, quizzes), and launch on platforms like Udemy or Teachable.

Potential earnings: $500-$5000+ per month, depending on your course's popularity and pricing.

17. **Freelance Photography** Got an eye for composition? Turn your photography hobby into a money-making side gig.

How to start: Build a portfolio, invest in decent equipment, and start marketing your services for events, portraits, or stock photography.

Potential earnings: $100-$500+ per shoot, or earn passively through stock photo sales.

18. **Virtual Event Planning** With the rise of remote work, virtual events are booming. If you're organized and tech-savvy, this could be your niche.

How to start: Familiarize yourself with virtual event platforms, create a service package, and start reaching out to businesses or individuals planning online events.

Potential earnings: $500-$2000+ per event, depending on size and complexity.

19. **App Development** Got coding skills? The app market is still growing. Create the next big thing or help businesses bring their app ideas to life.

How to start: Develop your coding skills, create a portfolio app, and start bidding on projects or launch your own app.

Potential earnings: $50-$150+ per hour for freelance work, or potentially much more if your own app takes off.

> 20. **Ghostwriting** Many people have stories to tell but lack the writing skills. That's where ghostwriters come in.

How to start: Hone your writing skills, perhaps specialize in a niche (memoirs, business books, etc.), and start looking for clients on freelancing platforms or by networking.
Potential earnings: $5000-$50000+ per book, depending on length and your experience.

> 21. **YouTube Content Creation** If you're comfortable on camera and have something interesting to share, YouTube could be your ticket to side hustle success.

How to start: Choose your niche, invest in basic equipment, start creating and uploading content regularly, and focus on building your audience.

Potential earnings: Varies widely, but successful YouTubers can earn $1000-$10000+ per month through ads, sponsorships, and merchandise.

> 22. **Transcription Services** Got fast, accurate typing skills? Transcription could be your calling. From medical to legal to general transcription, there's always a demand.

How to start: Take a transcription course, invest in transcription software, and look for gigs on platforms like Rev or TranscribeMe.

Potential earnings: $15-$30+ per hour, depending on your speed and the type of transcription.

> 23. **Resume Writing** In a competitive job market, a well-crafted resume can make all the difference. If you've got a way with words and understand what employers are looking for, this could be your niche.

How to start: Study current resume trends, create sample resumes, and start offering your services on job-related forums or LinkedIn.

Potential earnings: $100-$400+ per resume, depending on your experience and the client's level.

> 24. **Personal Training** (Online or In-Person) If you're a fitness buff, why not get paid to help others achieve their health goals?

How to start: Get certified, create workout plans, and start marketing your services. You can offer in-person training or tap into the growing online fitness market.

Potential earnings: $30-$100+ per hour, depending on your location and experience.

25. **Handmade Crafts** Etsy has made it easier than ever to turn your crafting hobby into a profitable side hustle.

How to start: Perfect your craft, take great photos of your products, set up an Etsy shop, and start promoting on social media.

Potential earnings: $500-$5000+ per month, depending on your products and marketing efforts.

26. **Website Flipping** Buy underperforming websites, improve them, and sell them for a profit. It's like house flipping, but digital.

How to start: Learn about website valuation, start small with a low-cost site, improve its content and monetization, then sell on platforms like Flippa.

Potential earnings: $1000-$10000+ per flip, depending on the website's potential and your improvements.

27. **Virtual Interior Design** Help people create their dream spaces without ever stepping foot in their homes.

How to start: Build a portfolio (you can start with your own space), learn to use 3D rendering software, and offer your services on freelancing platforms or social media.

Potential earnings: $50-$200+ per room design, depending on the complexity and your experience.

28. **Food Delivery** With the rise of apps like DoorDash and Uber Eats, it's easier than ever to make money delivering food in your spare time.

How to start: Sign up for one or more delivery apps, pass their background check, and start accepting orders.

Potential earnings: $15-$25+ per hour, including tips.

29. **Rent Out Your Car** If your car sits idle most of the time, why not make it work for you? Platforms like Turo allow you to rent out your vehicle to others.

How to start: List your car on a peer-to-peer car sharing platform, set your rates, and start accepting bookings. Potential earnings: $500-$1000+ per month, depending on your car and location.

30. **Translation Services** Fluent in more than one language? Translation services are always in demand.

How to start: Get certified if possible, create a portfolio of sample translations, and look for gigs on freelancing platforms or with translation agencies.

Potential earnings: $20-$50+ per hour, depending on the languages and type of translation.

31. **Lawn Care and Landscaping** If you've got a green thumb and don't mind physical work, this could be a lucrative side hustle.

How to start: Invest in basic equipment, start with neighbors and friends, and gradually expand your client base through word-of-mouth and local advertising.

Potential earnings: $25-$50+ per hour, depending on the services offered and your location.

32. **Podcasting Editing** Many aspiring podcasters have great content but lack the technical skills to produce a polished final product. That's where you come in.

How to start: Learn audio editing software, create sample edits, and offer your services on freelancing platforms or podcasting forums.

Potential earnings: $50-$200+ per episode, depending on length and complexity.

33. **Self-Publishing** Have a story to tell? With platforms like Amazon's Kindle Direct Publishing, it's easier than ever to become an author.

How to start: Write your book, hire an editor and cover designer (or do it yourself if you have the skills), and publish through a self-publishing platform.

Potential earnings: Highly variable, but successful self-published authors can make $1000-$10000+ per month.

34. **Dropservicing** Similar to dropshipping, but with services instead of products. You sell a service, then outsource the work to someone else.

How to start: Choose a service (like graphic design or writing), find reliable freelancers to do the work, and start marketing your services at a markup.

Potential earnings: $1000-$5000+ per month, depending on your services and client base.

35. **Microtasks** Platforms like Amazon Mechanical Turk offer small, quick tasks that can add up to decent money.

How to start: Sign up for microtask platforms, complete qualification tests if required, and start taking on tasks.
Potential earnings: $5-$20+ per hour, depending on your efficiency and the available tasks.
Remember, the key to side hustle success is finding something that aligns with your skills, interests, and available time. Don't be afraid to try multiple hustles until

you find the right fit. And always be on the lookout for ways to scale and automate your side gig to maximize your earnings.

> 36. **Virtual Fitness Instructor** With the rise of home workouts, there's a growing demand for online fitness instructors.

How to start: Get certified, create workout routines, set up a home studio, and start offering classes through platforms like Zoom or specialized fitness apps.

Potential earnings: $20-$100+ per class, depending on your expertise and class size.

> 37. **Social Media Influencer** If you've got a knack for creating engaging content and building a following, becoming an influencer could be your ticket to side hustle success.

How to start: Choose your niche, consistently create high-quality content, engage with your audience, and start reaching out to brands for collaborations.

Potential earnings: Highly variable, but successful micro-influencers can earn $500-$5000+ per post.

> 38. **3D Printing Services** Got a 3D printer? Turn it into a money-making machine by offering printing services.

How to start: Invest in a quality 3D printer, learn 3D modeling software, and start offering your services on platforms like Etsy or to local businesses.

Potential earnings: $20-$100+ per print, depending on size and complexity.

39. **Meal Prep Service** If you love cooking and are good at it, why not get paid to help busy professionals eat healthier?

How to start: Develop a menu, get necessary food handling certifications, and start marketing your services locally or through social media.

Potential earnings: $200-$500+ per week, depending on the number of clients and meals.

40. **Rent Out Storage Space** Got an empty garage or spare room? Turn it into a storage space for people in your area.

How to start: Clean and secure your space, list it on platforms like Neighbor.com, and start accepting renters. Potential earnings: $50-$400+ per month, depending on the size and location of your space.

41. **Mobile Car Detailing** Bring the car wash to your customers with a mobile detailing service.

How to start: Invest in quality cleaning supplies and portable equipment, create service packages, and start marketing to car owners in your area.

Potential earnings: $100-$200+ per detail job, depending on the level of service.

42. **Personal Chef Services** For those who can cook restaurant-quality meals, offering personal chef services can be a lucrative side gig.

How to start: Create a sample menu, get necessary food safety certifications, and start networking with potential clients or list your services on platforms like Thumbtack.

Potential earnings: $200-$500+ per event, depending on the number of people and complexity of the menu.

43. **Drone Photography/Videography** If you've got a drone and know how to use it, there's money to be made in aerial photography and videography.

How to start: Get certified (FAA certification in the US), practice your flying and photography skills, and start offering services for real estate, events, or stock footage.

Potential earnings: $100-$500+ per shoot, depending on the project scope.

44. **Rent Out Baby Gear** Parents traveling with young children often need to rent baby

equipment. If you've got baby gear collecting dust, why not rent it out?

How to start: Collect gently used baby equipment, ensure it meets safety standards, and list your items on platforms like BabyQuip.

Potential earnings: $100-$500+ per month, depending on your inventory and location.

45. **Book keeping Services** If you're good with numbers and organized, offering bookkeeping services to small businesses can be a profitable side hustle.

How to start: Get certified if possible, familiarize yourself with accounting software, and start offering your services to local small businesses or through freelancing platforms.
Potential earnings: $20-$50+ per hour, depending on your experience and the complexity of the work.

46. Bicycle Repair With the growing popularity of cycling, mobile bike repair services are in demand.

How to start: Learn bicycle repair skills (plenty of online resources available), invest in tools, and start offering your services locally.

Potential earnings: $50-$100+ per repair job, depending on the complexity.

> 47. **Sell Digital Products** Create and sell digital products like ebooks, templates, or printables.

How to start: Identify a need in your niche, create your digital product, and sell it through platforms like Etsy, your own website, or marketplaces like Creative Market.

Potential earnings: $500-$5000+ per month, depending on your products and marketing efforts.

> 48. **Become a Notary Public** Offer notary services in your spare time.

How to start: Complete your state's notary course, pass the exam, get your supplies, and start offering your services locally or through notary networks.

Potential earnings: $50-$200+ per signing session, depending on the type of document and your location.

> 49. **Pet Waste Removal** It's not glamorous, but it's a necessary service that many pet owners are willing to pay for.

How to start: Invest in basic equipment, create a service schedule, and start marketing to pet owners in your area.

Potential earnings: $25-$50+ per visit, with potential for recurring weekly or monthly clients.

> 50. **Become a Tour Guide** If you know your city well and love interacting with people, becoming a tour guide could be a fun and profitable side hustle.

How to start: Research your city's history and attractions, create unique tour itineraries, and start promoting your services through travel websites or local tourism offices.

Potential earnings: $50-$200+ per tour, depending on the length and number of participants.

There you have it, folks – 50 side hustles that can help you turn your spare time into cold, hard cash. But remember, this list is just the tip of the iceberg. The world of side hustles is constantly evolving, and new opportunities are popping up all the time.

The key is to find something that aligns with your skills, interests, and available time. Don't be afraid to experiment with different hustles until you find the right fit. And always be on the lookout for ways to scale and automate your side gig to maximize your earnings.

Now, I know what you're thinking: "This all sounds great, but how do I actually get started?" Well, buckle up, because in the next chapter, we're going to dive into a step-by-step guide on how to launch your side hustle and start bringing in that sweet, sweet extra cash. Are you ready to stop dreaming and start doing? Let's go!

Cap 4

From Zero to $1000: Your First Month's Gameplan

Alright, future moguls, it's time to put the rubber to the road. You've got your list of potential side hustles, you've got that fire in your belly, and you're ready to start raking in the cash. But where do you start? How do you go from zero to $1000 in your first month?

Let's break it down into a step-by-step gameplan that'll have you side hustling like a pro in no time.

Step 1: Choose Your Hustle First things first, you need to

pick your poison. Look
back at the list of 50 side hustles and choose one that:
a) Aligns with your skills and interests b) Fits your available time c) Has potential in your local market or online niche

Don't overthink this step. Remember, you're not married

to this hustle. If it doesn't work out, you can always pivot to something else. The important thing is to start.

Step 2: Do Your Research Once you've chosen your hustle, it's time to become an expert. Dive deep into:

- Market demand: Is there a need for your service or product?
- Competition: Who else is doing this? How can you differentiate yourself?
- Pricing: What are others charging? How much do you need to charge to make it worth your time?
- Legal requirements: Do you need any licensesor permits?

Knowledge is power, people. The more you know about your chosen hustle, the better positioned you'll be for success.

Step 3: Set Up Shop Now it's time to get your hustle off

the ground. This
might involve:

- Creating a basic web site or social media presence
- Setting up profiles on relevant platforms (Upwork, Etsy, Airbnb, etc.)
- Investing in necessary equipment or supplies
- Creating sample work or a portfolio

Don't get bogged down in perfectionism here. Your setup doesn't need to be perfect; it just needs to be functional. You can always improve and refine as you go.

Step 4: Create Your Offer

What exactly are you selling? Get specific about:

- Your services or products
- Your pricing structure
- Your unique selling proposition (What makes you different from the competition?)

Remember, you're not just selling a product or service; you're selling a solution to a problem. Frame your offer in terms of the benefits it provides to your customers.

Step 5: Start Marketing Time to get the word out! Some ways to start marketing your side hustle:

- Leverage your personal network (friends, family, colleagues)
- Use social media to show case your work and engage with potential customers
- Offer introductory discounts or promotions to attract your first clients
- Collaborate with complementary businesses or influencers in your niche

Don't be shy about self-promotion. If you don't believe in your hustle, who will?

Step 6: Deliver Excellence Once you start getting clients or customers, it's time to wow them. Go above and beyond to:

- Deliver high-quality work
- Provide excellent customer service
- Ask for feedback and continually improve

Remember, happy customers lead to repeat business and referrals – both crucial for growing your side hustle.

Step 7: Track and Optimize As you start bringing in some cash, it's important to keep track of:

- Your income and expenses
- Your time investment
- What's working and what's not

Use this data to continually refine and optimize your hustle. Maybe you need to raise your prices, focus on a specific type of client, or streamline your processes.

Now, let's put this all together into a 30-day gameplan:

Days 1-3: Choose Your Hustle and Research

- Pick your side hustle
- Deep dive into market research
- Identify your target audience

Days 4-7: Set Up Shop

- Create your online presence
- Invest in necessary equipment/supplies

- Develop your initial offer

Days 8-14: Start Marketing

- Reach out to your network
- Create and share content on socialmedia
- Offer an introductory promotion

Days 15-28: Hustle Hard

- Actively seek clients/customers
- Deliver excellent work
- Ask for feedback and testimonials

Days 29-30: Review and Optimize

- Analyze your first month's performance
- Identify are as for improvement
- Set goals for month two

Now, I know what you're thinking: "But Claude, how am I supposed to make $1000 in just 30 days?" Well, let's break it down with some examples:

Freelance Writing:

- Write 10 blog posts at $100 each = $1000

Virtual Assistant:

- 25 hours of work at $40/hour = $1000

Dog Walking:

- Walk 10 dogs per week at $25 per walk for 4 weeks = $1000

Etsy Shop:

- Sell 50 items at an average profit of $20 each = $1000

Remember, $1000 is just a target. You might make more, you might make less. The important thing is to start and gain momentum.

But here's the kicker: your first month probably won't be easy. You'll face rejection. You'll make mistakes. You'll wonder if this whole side hustle thing is worth it. But let me tell you something: every successful entrepreneur has been where you are right now. The difference between those who make it and those who don't isn't talent or luck – it's persistence.

So when the going gets tough (and it will), remember why you started this journey. Remember the freedom, the extra cash, the sense of accomplishment that comes from building something of your own. Keep pushing, keep learning, keep hustling.

And here's a little secret: even if you don't hit that $1000 mark in your first month, you'll have gained something even more valuable – experience. You'll have taken the first steps on your entrepreneurial journey. You'll have skills and knowledge that you didn't have before. And you'll be that much closer to building the life you want.

So, are you ready to turn your spare time into cold, hard cash? Are you prepared to join the ranks of the side hustle elite? Then what are you waiting for? Get out there and start hustling!
In the next chapter, we'll talk about how to scale your side hustle and take it to the next level. Because once you've tasted success, trust me, you're going to want more.

Let's keep this momentum going!

Cap 5

Scaling Up: Turn Your Side Hustle into a Cash Cow

Alright, hustlers, pat yourselves on the back. You've made it through your first month, and hopefully, you've got a taste of that sweet side hustle success. But here's the thing: we're not stopping there. Oh no, we're just getting started. It's time to take your side hustle to the next level and turn it into a bonafide cash cow.

Now, before we dive in, let's get one thing straight: scaling isn't just about working more hours. If that were the case, you'd be better off getting a second job. No, scaling is about working smarter, not harder. It's about leveraging your time, skills, and resources to exponentially increase your income without proportionally increasing your workload.

So, how do we do that? Let's break it down:

1. Automate Everything You Can

Time is your most precious resource. The more you can automate, the more time you'll have to focus on high-value tasks that actually grow your business.

Some areas to consider automating:

- Social media posting (use tools like Hootsuite or Buffer)
- Email responses (set up canned responses for common inquiries)
- Invoicing and payments (use accounting software like QuickBooks or FreshBooks)
- Customer on boarding (create a standardized welcome packet or video)

Remember, every minute you save on repetitive tasks is a minute you can spend on growing your business.

2. Out source Low-Value Tasks

There comes a point where your time becomes too valuable to spend on certain tasks. That's when it's time to start outsourcing.

Consider outsourcing things like:

- Administrative tasks (hire a virtual assistant)
- Content creation (use freelance writers or designers)
- Customer service (use a call center service)
- Book keeping (hire a part-time book keeper)

Yes, outsourcing costs money. But if it frees you up to take on more high-paying work or to focus on business development, it's worth the investment.

3. Diversify Your Offerings

Don't put all your eggs in one basket. Look for ways to expand your services or product line to increase your income streams.

For example:

- If you're a freelance writer, start offering editing services as well
- If you're selling hand made products on Etsy, create digital patterns or tutorials
- If you're a virtual assistant, offer package deals for ongoing services

The key is to find complementary offerings that appeal to your existing customer base.

4. Raise Your Rates

As you gain experience and build a reputation, don't be afraid to raise your rates. Many side hustlers undervalue their services, especially when starting out.

How to raise your rates without losing clients:

- Gradually increase rates for new clients
- Offer additional value to justify the increase
- Give long-term clients advance notice and consider grandfathering them in at a lower rate

Remember, you're not just selling your time; you're selling your expertise and the results you deliver.

5. Focus on Repeat Business and Referrals

It's much easier (and cheaper) to keep existing clients than to constantly find new ones. Focus on delivering exceptional value to encourage repeat business and referrals.

Strategies to encourage loyalty:

- Offer loyalty discounts or rewards programs
- Ask for referrals and offer incentives for successful ones
- Stay in touch with past clients through email newsletters or social media

Word-of-mouth marketing is powerful and free - leverage it!

6. Create Passive Income Streams

The holy grail of scaling is creating income streams that don't require your constant attention. This could include:

- Creating and selling digital products (ebooks, courses, templates)
- Affiliate marketing
- Building a membership site
- Developing a mobile app

While these often require significant upfront work, they can generate income long after you've created them.

7. Leverage Technology

Use technology to reach more customers and streamline your operations. This might include:

- Building a mobile app for your service
- Using chatbots for customer service
- Implementing a CRM system to manage customer relationships
- Using project management tools to improve efficiency

The right tech tools can help you serve more customers without working more hours.

8. Build a Team

At some point, you might need to transition from a one-person show to a small team. This could mean:

- Hiring part-time or freelance help
- Partnering with other professionals in your field
- Creating a network of subcontractors

Building a team allows you to take on more work and offer a wider range of services.

9. Focus on Your Unique Selling Proposition (USP)

As you scale, it's crucial to differentiate yourself from the competition. Identify what makes you unique and double down on it.

Your USP could be:

- Specialized expertise in a particular niche
- Exceptional customer service
- Innovative technology or processes
- Aunique style or approach

Whatever it is, make sure it's clear in all your marketing and branding.

10. Invest in Marketing

As you grow, you'll need to reach beyond your personal network. This might mean:

- Investing in paid advertising (GoogleAds, Facebook Ads, etc.)
- Hiring a PR firm
- Attending industry events or trade shows
- Collaborating with influencers in your niche

Remember, marketing is an investment, not an expense. Track your ROI and double down on what works.

Now, let's put this all together into a 90-day scaling plan:

Days 1-30: Streamline and Optimize

- Identify tasks to automate or out source
- Implement productivity tools and systems
- Review and optimize your pricing strategy

Days 31-60: Expand and Diversify

- Develop new offerings or products
- Implement a referral program
- Start building passive income streams

Days 61-90: Scale and Grow

- Invest in targeted marketing efforts
- Start building a team or network of partners
- Focus on scaling your most profitable offerings

Remember, scaling is a process, not an event. It takes time, effort, and often some trial and error. But with persistence and the right strategies, you can turn your side hustle into a serious money-making machine. But here's the thing: as you start to scale, you'll face new challenges. You'll need to manage your time more effectively. You'll need to deal with the feast-and-famine cycles that often come with freelancing or entrepreneurship. You'll need to handle the mental stress of taking bigger risks and dealing with more responsibility.

That's why it's crucial to not lose sight of why you started this journey in the first place. Is it for the extra cash? The freedom? The sense of accomplishment? Whatever your reasons, keep them front and center as you grow. And remember, scaling doesn't mean you have to turn your side hustle into a full-time gig (unless you want to, of course). The beauty of a side hustle is that you can scale it to whatever level fits your lifestyle and goals.

So, are you ready to take your side hustle to the next level? Are you prepared to stop thinking small and start building an empire? Then it's time to implement these strategies and watch your side hustle soar.

In the next chapter, we'll talk about something that often gets overlooked in the world of side hustles: the dark side. Because let's face it, it's not all rainbows and unicorns out there. There are pitfalls, challenges, and potential downsides that you need to be aware of. But don't worry - we'll also talk about how to navigate these challenges and come out on top. Stay tuned, hustlers!

Cap 6

The Dark Side of Side Hustles: What They Don't Tell You

Alright, aspiring moguls, it's time for a reality check. We've talked about the glitz and glamour of side hustles - the extra cash, the freedom, the thrill of building something of your own. But now it's time to pull back the curtain and look at the darker side of the hustle life.

Don't get me wrong - I'm not here to rain on your parade or discourage you from pursuing your side hustle dreams. But if you're going to succeed in this game, you need to go in with your eyes wide open. So, let's dive into the nitty-gritty, the stuff that those Instagram "entrepreneurs" conveniently leave out of their perfectly curated posts.

1. The Time Suck

Let's start with the obvious: side hustles take time. A lot of time. And not just the time you spend actually doing the work. There's also:

- Marketing and self-promotion
- Dealing with clients or customers
- Book keeping and administrative tasks
- Learning new skills
- Trouble shooting problems

Before you know it, your "spare time" has vanished. Your Netflix queue is gathering dust, your friends are wondering if you've fallen off the face of the earth, and you can't remember the last time you had a full night's sleep.

The Reality Check: Be prepared to sacrifice some of your free time, especially in the beginning. Set clear boundaries and learn to prioritize ruthlessly.

2. The Emotional Rollercoaster

One day you're on top of the world, landing a big client or making a killer sale. The next day you're in the dumps, dealing with a difficult customer or facing a dry spell in business.

Side hustling can be an emotional rollercoaster, and it's not for the faint of heart. You'll face:

- Rejection and criticism
- Imposter syndrome
- Financial stress
- The pressure of being solely responsible for your success

The Reality Check: Develop a thick skin and a strong support system. Learn to separate your self-worth from your business success.

3. The Financial Uncertainty

Sure, the potential for extra income is there. But so is the potential for:

- Unpredictable income
- Unexpected expenses
- Late-paying clients
- Slow periods in business

And let's not forget - you might actually lose money, especially in the beginning when you're investing in equipment, marketing, or inventory.

The Reality Check: Have a financial cushion and a solid budgeting system. Don't quit your day job until your side hustle income is stable and substantial.

4. The Work-Life Imbalance

Remember when we talked about escaping the 9-5 grind? Well, welcome to the 24/7 hustle. When you're running a side business, it can be hard to switch off. You might find yourself:

- Checking emails at all hours
- Working weekends and holidays
- Neglecting your health and relationships
- Feeling guilty when you're not working

The Reality Check: Set clear work hours and stick to them. Learn to say no and prioritize self-care.

5. The Legal and Tax Headaches

Ah, the glamorous world of self-employment taxes and business regulations. Depending on your side hustle, you might need to deal with:

- Registering your business
- Getting necessary licenses or permits
- Keeping meticulous records for tax purposes
- Paying quarterly estimated taxes
- Understanding and complying with relevant laws and regulations

The Reality Check: Do your research and consider consulting with a lawyer or accountant. The penalties for non-compliance can be steep.

6. The Isolation

Side hustling can be a lonely gig, especially if you're used to working in a team environment. You might miss:

- Watercooler chats with colleagues
- Bouncing ideas off others
- Having a built-in support system at work

The Reality Check: Make an effort to network with other entrepreneurs. Join online communities or local meetups in your industry.

7. The Creativity Drain

When your passion becomes your job, it can sometimes suck the joy out of it. You might find:

- The pressure to monetize kills your creativity
- You start to resent something you once loved
- You're too exhausted from your side hustle to pursue other hobbies

The Reality Check: Make time for creative pursuits that aren't tied to making money. Remember why you started this journey in the first place.

8. The Skills Gap

You might be great at your core skill - whether that's writing, designing, coding, or whatever. But running a business requires a whole other set of skills:

- Marketing and sales
- Financial management
- Customer service
- Project management
- Negotiation

The Reality Check: Be prepared for a steep learning curve. Invest in developing your business skills alongside your technical skills.

9. The Competition Crush

In today's digital age, you're not just competing with local businesses. You're potentially competing with everyone in the world who offers a similar product or service. This can lead to:

- Race-to-the-bottompricing
- Difficulty standing out in a crowded market
- Constant pressure to innovate and improve

The Reality Check: Focus on your unique value proposition. Don't try to compete on price alone.

10. The Burnout Risk

With all of the above factors combined, burnout is a real risk for side hustlers. Signs of burnout include:

- Chronic fatigue
- Decreased motivation
- Increased irritability
- Declining quality of work
- Physical symptoms like headaches or insomnia

The Reality Check: Listen to your body and mind. Take breaks, set boundaries, and don't be afraid to scale back if needed.

Now, I know what you're thinking. "Geez, Claude, way to be a buzzkill. Why would anyone want to start a side hustle after reading all that?"

Well, here's the thing: knowledge is power. By being aware of these potential pitfalls, you can prepare for them and navigate around them. And remember, for every dark side, there's a bright side too:

- The time suck? It's also an opportunity to develop incredible time management skills.
- The emotional rollercoaster? It's building your resilience and emotional intelligence.
- The financial uncertainty? It's teaching you valuable money management skills.
- The work-life imbalance? It's forcing you to prioritize what's truly important in your life.
- The legal and tax headaches? They're giving you a crash course in business operations.
- The isolation? It's pushing you to build a network and community of like-minded individuals.
- The creativity drain? It's challenging you to find new sources of inspiration and innovation.
- The skills gap? It's an opportunity for continuous learning and personal growth.
- The competition crush? It's motivating you to up your game and truly excel in your field.
- The burn out risk? It's teaching you the importance of self-care and balance.

The key is to go into your side hustle journey with your eyes wide open. Expect challenges, prepare for them, and have strategies in place to overcome them.

Remember, every successful entrepreneur has faced these dark sides and come out the other side. The difference between those who make it and those who don't isn't the absence of challenges - it's the ability to persist in the face of them.

So, are you still ready to hustle? Are you prepared to face the dark side and come out stronger? If so, then you've got what it takes to turn your side gig into a success story.

In the next chapter, we'll tackle another not-so-sexy but crucial aspect of side hustling: the legal and financial stuff. We'll break down the boring but important details you need to know to keep your hustle legit and your finances in check. Stay with me, hustlers - we're in the home stretch now!

Cap 7
Taxes, Legalities, and Other Boring Stuff You Can't Ignore

Alright, hustlers, I know this isn't the sexy part of running a side gig. You'd probably rather be creating content, closing deals, or counting your cash. But ignore this chapter at your peril. The boring stuff we're about to dive into could be the difference between a thriving side hustle and a legal or financial nightmare.

So, put on your adulting hat, grab a coffee (or something stronger), and let's tackle the nitty-gritty of taxes, legalities, and other essential but yawn-inducing aspects of your side hustle.

1. Choosing Your Business Structure

First things first: what kind of business entity are you? This isn't just a philosophical question - it has real implications for your taxes, liability, and paperwork.

Your main options are:

- Sole Propriet or ship: The simple ststructure, but offers no personal liability protection.
- Limited Liability Company (LLC): Offers liability protection and tax flexibility.

- Corporation: More complex, but can offer additional benefits for larger businesses.

For most side hustlers, a sole proprietorship or single-member LLC is sufficient. But consult with a lawyer or accountant to determine what's best for your specific situation.

2. Registering Your Business

Depending on your location and business type, you might need to:

- Register your business name (DBA - "Doing Business As")
- Get a federal Employer Identification Number (EIN)
- Register for state and local taxes
- Obtain necessary licenses or permits

Check with your local Small Business Administration (SBA) office or chamber of commerce for specific requirements in your area.

3. Keeping Records

I know, I know - bookkeeping is about as exciting as watching paint dry. But trust me, future you will thank present you for keeping meticulous records. You'll need to track:

- Income from all sources

- Business expenses
- Receipts and invoices
- Mileage (if you use your vehicle for business)
- Home office expenses (if applicable)

Consider using accounting software like QuickBooks, FreshBooks, or Wave to make this easier. Your sanity (and your accountant) will thank you.

4. Understanding Self-Employment Taxes

Welcome to the world of self-employment taxes! As a side hustler, you're now responsible for both the employee and employer portions of Social Security and Medicare taxes. That means you'll be paying 15.3% in addition to your regular income tax.

But don't panic - you can deduct half of your self-employment tax when calculating your adjusted gross income. And remember, you only pay self-employment tax on net earnings of $400 or more.

5. Estimated Tax Payments

If you expect to owe $1,000 or more in taxes for your side hustle, you'll need to make quarterly estimated tax payments. The due dates are:

- April 15
- June 15
- September 15
- January 15 of the following year

Failing to make these payments can result in penalties, so mark those dates in your calendar!

6. Deductions: Your New Best Friend

Now for some good news: as a business owner, you can deduct ordinary and necessary business expenses. This might include:

- Home office expenses
- Equipment and supplies
- Professional development (courses, conferences, etc.)
- Marketing and advertising costs
- Travel expenses related to your business
- Health insurance premiums

Keep in mind that meals and entertainment expenses are only 50% deductible, and commuting costs generally aren't deductible at all.

7. The 1099 Form

If you earn $600 or more from a single client in a year, they should send you a 1099 form. But even if they don't, you're still responsible for reporting that income. Don't think you can fly under the radar - the IRS has ways of finding out, and the penalties for underreporting income can be steep.

8. Separating Personal and Business Finances

Do yourself a favor and open a separate bank account for your side hustle. This will make it much easier to track business income and expenses, and it'll look a lot more professional to your clients.

Consider getting a business credit card too - it can help you build business credit and make it easier to track expenses.

9. Insurance Considerations

Depending on your side hustle, you might need additional insurance coverage. This could include:

- General liability insurance
- Professional liability insurance (also known as errors and omissions insurance)
- Product liability insurance
- Commercial property insurance

Don't assume your personal insurance policies will cover your business activities - they probably won't.

10. Contracts and Agreements

Get everything in writing. Whether it's a client agreement, a partnership agreement, or terms of service for your website, clear contracts can save you a world of headache down the line.
Consider having a lawyer review your contracts, especially as your side hustle grows.

11. Intellectual Property Protection

If your side hustle involves creating original work (writing, design, inventions, etc.), you'll want to understand and protect your intellectual property rights. This might involve:

- Copyrights
- Trademarks
- Patents

While these protections can be complex and sometimes expensive, they're crucial for protecting your creative work.

12. Privacy and Data Protection

If you're collecting any customer data (even just email addresses for a mailing list), you need to be aware of privacy laws. This includes:

- Having a clear privacy policy on your website
- Securing customer data
- Complying with regulations like GDPR if you have European customers

Data breaches can be costly, both financially and in terms of reputation damage.

13. Employment Laws

If your side hustle grows to the point where you're hiring help, you'll need to understand employment laws. This includes:

- Proper classification of employees vs independent contractors
- Minimum wage and over time regulations
- Anti-discrimination laws
- Work places afety requirements

Misclassifying workers or violating labor laws can result in hefty fines, so tread carefully here.

14. Zoning Laws and Home-Based Business Regulations

If you're running your side hustle from home, check your local zoning laws. Some areas have restrictions on home-based businesses, especially if you'll have clients coming to your home or if you're selling physical products.

15. Industry-Specific Regulations

Depending on your side hustle, you might be subject to industry-specific regulations. For example:

- Food businesses need to comply with health department regulations
- Financial advisors need to be properly licensed
- Child care providers of ten need special certifications

Do your research to make sure you're complying with all relevant regulations in your field.

Now, I know what you're thinking. "Claude, my eyes are glazing over. Do I really need to worry about all this stuff for my little side gig?"

The short answer is: yes. The long answer is: yes, and it's in your best interest to get this stuff right from the start.

Here's why:

1. It protects you legally. The right business structure and insurance can shield your personal assets if something goes wrong.
2. It saves you money in the long run. Proper record-keeping and understanding of tax deductions can significantly reduce your tax bill.
3. It sets you up for growth. If you ever want to scale your side hustle into a full-time business, having your legal and financial ducks in a row will make that transition much smoother.
4. It gives you peace of mind. Knowing you're operating legally and ethically means one less thing to worry about as you build your empire.

Now, I'm not suggesting you need to become an expert in business law or accounting overnight. But you do need to have a basic understanding of these issues and know when to seek professional help.

Consider this your wake-up call. If you've been flying by the seat of your pants with your side hustle, it's time to get serious. Set aside some time to:

1. Research the specific legal and tax requirements for your type of business in your location.
2. Set up a proper book keeping system.
3. Consult with a lawyer and an accountant (many offer free initial consultations).
4. Create a compliance check list for your business.

Remember, ignorance is not bliss when it comes to legal and financial matters. The IRS, your state government, and potential litigants don't care if you "didn't know" you were supposed to do something.

But don't let this scare you off. Millions of people successfully navigate these waters every day. With a little education and the right professional help when needed, you can too.

In the next chapter, we'll look at ways to work smarter, not harder. We'll explore strategies for automation and outsourcing that can help you scale your side hustle without working yourself to death. Stay tuned, hustlers - the best is yet to come!

Cap 8

Work Smarter, Not Harder: Automation and Outsourcing

Listen up, wage slaves! If you think hustling means working yourself to death, you're doing it wrong. This chapter is all about maximizing your profits while minimizing your effort. Because let's face it, you're not getting any younger, and neither is your liver. It's time to embrace the art of doing less and earning more. Buckle up, buttercup – we're about to turn you into a lean, mean, profit-making machine.

Automation: Your New Best Friend

Remember when your parents told you robots would take your job? Well, it's time to embrace the robot overlords and let them work for you. Here are some ways to automate your side hustle and reclaim your precious time:

- Social Media Management: Use tools like Buffer or Hootsuite to schedule your posts. Because who has time to tweet while they're hustling? Set it and forget it, like that rotisserie chicken you bought and never ate.
- Email Marketing: Set up automated email sequences with MailChimp or ConvertKit. It's like having a salesperson who never sleeps, never asks for a raise, and never steals your lunch from the office fridge.

- Chatbots: Let AI handle customer service while you're busy counting your money. Just don't blame me when they become sentient and take over your business. At least you'll have more time for panic room planning.
- Project Management: Tools like Trello or Asana can keep your tasks organized without you lifting a finger. It's like having a personal assistant who doesn't judge your 3 AM ice cream binges.
- Invoicing and Payments: Use services like QuickBooks or FreshBooks to automate your billing. Because chasing payments is about as fun as a root canal, and twice as expensive.
- Content Creation: Yes, even your witty blog posts can be semi-automated with tools like Jasper.ai. Just add your personal touch, or don't. We won't tell if you won't.

Outsourcing: Because You Can't Do Everything (And You Shouldn't)

Still doing your own grunt work? That's cute. Here's how to delegate like a boss and free up your time for more important things, like perfecting your martini recipe:

- Virtual Assistants: Hire someone in a developing country to do your admin work for peanuts. Is it ethical? Who cares! It's capitalism, baby! Just remember, karma's a bitch, and so is your new VA if you don't pay them on time.
- Freelancers: Use platforms like Upwork or Fiverr to find skilled professionals. Just remember, you

get what you pay for. So if you pay in exposure, expect work that looks like it was done by a blind monkey on a unicycle. In a hurricane.

- Family and Friends: Exploit your loved ones' labor! Nothing says "I care" like underpaying your relatives. Who needs Christmas dinner invitations anyway?

- Interns: Ah, the time-honored tradition of free labor disguised as "experience." Just make sure they're learning something, like how to make the perfect latte for their future corporate overlords.

- Specialized Services: For tasks that require expertise, like legal or accounting work, hire professionals. It's cheaper than bail or an IRS audit, trust me.

The Art of Delegation: Making Others Do Your Bidding
Now that you know who to outsource to, let's talk about how to do it without coming off as a complete sociopath:

- Clear Communication: Be specific about what you want. "Make it pop" is not a valid instruction, Karen.
- Set Deadlines: But make them realistic. Rome wasn't built in a day, and your e-commerce empire won't be either.
- Provide Resources: Give your minions – I mean, team members – the tools they need to succeed. It's like feeding a fish so you can eat for a lifetime, or something like that.

- Feedback Loop: Regular check-ins keep projects on track. It's also a great opportunity to practice your "disappointed but not surprised" face.
- Learn to Let Go: Micromanaging is so last season. Embrace the chaos and trust the process. What's the worst that could happen? (Don't answer that.)

Optimizing Your Workflow: Because Efficiency is Sexy
Now that you've automated and outsourced, it's time to fine-tune your own workflow. Here's how to squeeze every last drop of productivity out of your day:

1. Time Blocking: Schedule your day like a boss. And by boss, I mean someone who actually knows what they're doing.
2. The Pomodoro Technique: Work in focused bursts with short breaks. It's like HIIT for your brain, minus the sweat and regret.
3. Batching Similar Tasks: Group like activities together. It's more efficient and gives you the illusion of accomplishment.
4. Eliminating Distractions: Put your phone on silent, close those 47 browser tabs, and for the love of all that is holy, stop checking your ex's Instagram.
5. Learning to Say No: Not every opportunity is a good one. Sometimes, the most productive thing you can do is absolutely nothing.

Remember, the goal is to create a system where money flows into your pocket while you sit on a beach sipping overpriced cocktails.

If you're not working towards that, you're just a sucker with a hobby. And let's be honest, your macaroni art isn't going to pay the bills.

In conclusion, work smarter, not harder. Automate what you can, outsource what you can't, and spend your newfound free time doing what you love – like scrolling through social media and judging other people's life choices. Because that's what true success looks like, right?

Now go forth and conquer, you lazy, brilliant bastards. The world is your oyster, and thanks to automation and outsourcing, you don't even have to shuck it yourself.

Cap 9

The Side Hustle Lifestyle: Balancing Hustle and Life

Alright, you money-hungry maniacs, it's time to talk about the elephant in the room - your pathetic attempt at having a life while chasing that sweet, sweet side hustle cash. You thought you could have it all, didn't you? Make bank on the side, keep your day job, maintain relationships, and maybe even remember to shower occasionally. How's that working out for you?

Let's face it, your work-life balance is about as stable as a Jenga tower after a few rounds of tequila. But fear not, you overworked, under-showered hustlers. This chapter is here to show you how to juggle your side gig, your day job, and that thing called a personal life without completely losing your mind (or your friends, family, and will to live).

The Myth of Work-Life Balance First things first, let's

shatter that delusion you've been clinging to. There's no such thing as perfect work-life balance. It's a lie sold to you by lifestyle gurus who've never had to choose between meeting a deadline and attending their kid's school play. The sooner you accept this harsh reality, the sooner you can stop beating yourself up and start working on a lifestyle that doesn't make you want to scream into the void every other Tuesday.

Signs You're Failing at Life (While Succeeding at Hustling)

Before we dive into solutions, let's take a moment to recognize the signs that your hustle has taken over your life:

1. Your pets have filed a missing person report on you.
2. Your Tinder bio reads "CEO of 3 startups, 2 side hustles, and 0 free time."
3. You've started dreaming in spreadsheets.
4. Your idea of a vacation is working from a different coffee shop.
5. You've forgotten what your friends look like without the Zoom filter.

If you nodded along to three or more of these, congratulations! You're officially a workaholic disaster. But don't worry, there's hope for you yet (maybe).

The Art of Saying "No" (Without Being a Total Jerk)

Here's a revolutionary concept for you overachievers: you don't have to say yes to everything. I know, mind-blowing, right? Your time is valuable, and every "yes" to a new project or commitment is a "no" to something else - like sleep, sanity, or basic hygiene.

Try these on for size: "I'd love to, but I'm fully booked right now. Have you considered asking someone who cares?" "Thanks for thinking of me, but I'm prioritizing my mental health over your project." "That sounds like an amazing opportunity for someone else."

Remember, "No" is a complete sentence. You don't owe anyone an explanation for why you can't take on their soul-sucking project.

Scheduling Your Life Like a Boss (Because You Are One, Aren't You?)
If you're not treating your personal life with the same obsessive attention you give your side hustle, you're doing it wrong. It's time to schedule the hell out of your life:

1. Sleep: Yes, it's necessary. No, RedBull is not a substitute.
2. Exercise: So you don't die before you can enjoy your millions.
3. Relationships: Remember those people who liked you before you had a side hustle? Yeah, them.
4. Self-care: Take a shower, for the love of all that is holy.
5. Hobbies: Preferably something that doesn't involve a screen or making money.

Block out time for these in your calendar and treat them with the same respect you'd give a client meeting. Your future, slightly less burned-out self will thank you.

The 80/20 Rule of Not Losing Your Mind You've probably

heard of the Pareto Principle: 80% of
your results come from 20% of your efforts. Apply this to your side hustle and life:

1. Identify the 20% of your hustle activities that bring in 80% of your revenue. Focus on those.
2. Figure out the 20% of your personal life that brings you 80% of your joy. Prioritize it.
3. Ruthlessly cutor delegate the rest.

This includes that high-maintenance client who pays peanuts but demands the world. Cut them loose - they're the reason you cry in the shower (when you actually find time to shower).

Outsourcing Your Life (Because You Can't Clone Yourself...Yet)

If you're not outsourcing, you're playing small. Here's what you can (and should) outsource:

1. House hold chores: Cleaning, laundry, grocery shopping. There's an app for that.
2. Administrative tasks: Email management, scheduling, data entry. Get a virtual assistant.

3. Meal prep: Because cereal for dinner every night is sad, even for you.
4. Dog walking: Your furbaby deserves better than your neglect.
5. Personal shopping: Let someone else figure out what clothes still fit your work-from-home body.

Yes, it costs money. But time is money, and sanity is priceless.

The Art of Multitasking (Without Destroying Your Brain)

Despite what productivity gurus tell you, multitasking is sometimes necessary. The trick is to do it strategically:

1. Pair mindless tasks with brain-intensive ones: Listen to work-related podcasts while doing chores.
2. Use commute time wisely: Take calls or dictate ideas while driving (hands-free, please).
3. Work out your body and your business: Take walking meetings or brainstorm while on the treadmill.

Just don't try to close a deal while changing a diaper. Trust me on this one.

Setting Boundaries (Before You Lose Your Mind) Your

clients, family, and friends will take as much as you're willing to give. It's up to you to set boundaries:

1. Establish work hours and stick to them. Yes, even for "urgent" requests.
2. Createa dedicated workspace. The couch is for Netflix, not for hustling.
3. Use separate phones or apps for work and personal life.
4. Learn to unplug. The world won't end if you don't check your email for a few hours.

And for the love of all that is holy, stop checking work messages on the toilet. It's unsanitary and sad.
Dealing with Burnout (Because It's Coming for You)

Burnout isn't just for corporate drones. It's coming for you too, side hustler. Know the signs:

1. You fantasize about your laptop spontaneously combusting.
2. The thought of another Zoom call makes you want to gouge out your eyes.
3. You can't remember the last time you felt genuinely excited about your work.

When burnout hits, don't ignore it. Take a real break. And no, working on a different project doesn't count as a break, you workaholic maniac.

Relationships: Remember Those? Newsflash: Your

significant other, friends, and family are
not just NPCs in the video game of your life. They're real

people who, for some reason, still want to spend time with you. Don't take them for granted:

1. Schedule regular date nights or friend hangouts. And be present, not checking your phone every two minutes.
2. Involve your loved ones in your side hustle when appropriate. They might actually have good ideas (shocking, I know).
3. Be honest about your commitments and limitations. They can't support you if they don't know what's going on.

Remember, success is pretty hollow if you have no one to share it with (except your cat, who only loves you for the fancy feast your side hustle money buys).

The Importance of Self-Care (No, Really) Self-care isn't just

for Instagram influencers. It's for hustlers like you who are one missed deadline away from a nervous breakdown. Make time for:

1. Mental Health: Therapy, meditation, or just staring at a wall in silence for 10 minutes.
2. Physical Health: Regular check-ups, exercise, and eating something that isn't coffee or takeout.
3. Hobbies: Remember those things you used to do for fun before the hustle consumed your soul?

Your side hustle should enhance your life, not replace it. If you're not taking care of yourself, you're just a hamster on a wheel, running faster and faster but going nowhere.

The Myth of "Having It All" Let's wrap this up with a hard

truth: you can't have it all.
At least not all at once. Life is about choices and trade-offs. Some days, you'll crush it at work but forget to call your mom. Other days, you'll have a great time with friends but fall behind on a project.

The key is to be intentional about your choices. Decide what truly matters to you and prioritize accordingly. And for heaven's sake, cut yourself some slack. You're trying to build an empire while maintaining a semblance of a life. It's not easy, and it's not supposed to be.

Remember why you started this side hustle in the first place. Was it for freedom? Financial security? Creative fulfillment? Don't lose sight of that goal in the daily grind. Your side hustle should be a means to an end, not the end itself.

So there you have it, you ambitious lunatics. The secret to balancing your side hustle and your life is that there is no perfect balance. It's a constant juggling act, and sometimes you'll drop the ball. The trick is to make sure you're dropping the right balls at the right time.

Now go forth and hustle, you beautiful disasters. Just remember to shower occasionally, call your mom, and maybe, just maybe, take a day off once in a while. Your empire will still be there tomorrow, but your sanity might not be if you don't take care of yourself.

And if all else fails, there's always the option of becoming a hermit and living in a cave. At least then you'd have an excuse for your poor hygiene and lack of social skills. Hustle on, you magnificent maniacs!

Stop Reading, Start Hustling

Alright, you money-hungry maniacs, we've reached the end of this rollercoaster ride through the world of side hustles. If you've made it this far without throwing your device across the room or starting seventeen new business ventures, congratulations – you have more self-control than a monk in a strip club.

Let's recap what we've learned on this wild journey, shall we?

1. Your 9-to-5 job is slowly sucking the life out of you, one soul-crushing meeting at a time.
2. The side hustle mindset is like a virus that infects your brain – but in a good way, like a financially beneficial zombie apocalypse.
3. There are at least 50 ways to make money on the side, and surprisingly, none of them involve selling your organs (though we didn't explicitly rule it out).
4. You can go from zero to hero (or at least to a thousand bucks) in just a month, assuming you're not too busy binge-watching Netflix.
5. Scaling up is possible, but it might cost you your sanity, your social life, and your ability to remember what day it is.
6. The dark side of side hustles exists, and it's not just the under-eye bags from lack of sleep – it's a whole new world of stress and potential failure.

7. Taxes and legalities are about as exciting as watching paint dry, but ignore them at your peril.
8. Automation and out sourcing are your tickets to freedom (and possibly world domination).
9. Balance is key, unless you en joy being a rich, lonely hermit with an impressive bank account and no one to share it with.

Now, here's the most crucial part of this conclusion, so pay attention, you wannabe entrepreneurs:
Stop. Reading. Start. Hustling. Yes, you heard me right. Put this damn book down (or close the e-reader, you tech-savvy minion). Knowledge
without action is about as useful as a chocolate teapot. You've got the tools, you've got the attitude, and you've got an unhealthy desire for more money. What are you waiting for? An engraved invitation from the universe? Get out there and start your side hustle. Make mistakes. Fail spectacularly.

Then pick yourself up, dust off your bruised ego, and try again. Because here's the dirty little secret about success: it's built on a mountain of failures, false starts, and "what the hell was I thinking" moments.

Remember, in the grand scheme of things, we're all just temporary visitors on this floating rock hurtling through space. You might as well make some cash and have fun while you're here. Your side hustle could be the key to financial freedom, or at least to affording that overpriced avocado toast you millennials seem to love so much.

And if all else fails, you can always write a book telling other people how to make money. It worked for me, didn't it? Just remember, if you do, I'll expect my cut for inspiring you. After all, hustling goes both ways.

Now go forth and conquer, you beautiful, money-hungry maniacs. The world is your oyster, and it's time to pry that sucker open and find your pearl. Or at least a shiny pebble you can sell on Etsy as a "rare, artisanal stone." And always remember: the best time to start was yesterday, the second-best time is now, and the worst time is after you've spent all your money on get-rich-quick schemes and motivational seminars. Sowhatareyoustilldoinghere?Gethustling!Your empire isn't going to build itself while you sit there reading. The next chapter of your life starts now – make it a bestseller.